WHAT REMAINS

WHAT REMAINS

POEMS BY

NICOLE DALCOURT

Blackbird Books 2025

FIRST EDITION

© 2025 Nicole Dalcourt
Published by Blackbird Books

Cover Art by John Gould:
Porphyry-Crowned Lorikeet (1804-1881)

ALL RIGHTS RESERVED

No part of this book may be reproduced without written permission from the author except for brief quotations or reviews.

For permission, inquiries or to contact author, please email nicole@nicoledalcourt.com

Library and Archives Canada Cataloging Publication:
Title: What Remains / Nicole Dalcourt
Names: Dalcourt, Nicole, author
ISBN 978-1-0695858-0-6 (softcover)
Subjects: Poetry

This book is dedicated to my mother, my biggest teacher and my greatest lesson.

I love you.

AUTHOR'S NOTE

I feel like I've been grieving for most of my life, and only a small portion of that grief has been about death. I have lived through the often complicated grief of mourning the living, the loss of relationships with people I love, and finally realizing I am equally to blame for some of the things I have lost.

This collection of poetry is not an indictment against the people who are in it. It is a personal exploration of memory, emotion and growth. The people who appear in these poems are part of the landscape of my life and were part of the moments that shaped me. If you find yourself in these lines, know that it is with honesty and humanity, not resentment. We all do what we need to survive and I hope this collection opens a window, instead of a wound.

CONTENTS

PART ONE:

I Told No One and Still It Is True	3
Summer at My Nana's Turquoise House	4
Inhobbak	5
Childhood Fragments	6
September 1988	8
Last Childhood Summer	9
Bible Belt	10
I Measured My Life in Summers	11
How to Ask for Help	12
Two Sparrows in a Hurricane	14
Two Sparrows	15
Sixteen	16
The Brave One	17
An Inventory of Night	19
Where it Hurts When You're Alive	20

PART TWO:

On The Side of a Country Road	23
The Lilac Tree is Burning	24

The Weight of a Marriage in Trouble	25
You Don't Have to Be a Saint to Talk to God	26
The Last Supper	27
Before & After	29
Holy Ground	30
I'm Not Dying, It Just Feels Like It	31
A Year After Our Divorce	32
A Year After	34
Wild Horses	36
So Much Living to Do	37
Lovers in August	38
The Way You Love Me	39
Reasons I Married My Second Husband	40
Born in the Kitchen	41

PART THREE:

Let the Fire Come	45
Threshold	46
Nothing Stays the Same	47
No One's Daughter	48
What My Father Grew	49
Notes From the Backyard	50
Acceptance Wears a Summer Dress	51

The Space Between Dreaming	52
Dreaming	53
In the Longing of This Body	54
My Father's Grave	55
Forest Church	57
This Morning	58
The Summer I Became a God	59
Cleanse	60
Notes & Acknowledgments	63

Part One

What is it about childhood that never lets you go?

– Mitch Albom

Part One

I TOLD NO ONE AND STILL IT IS TRUE

I am small,
growing beside a river
until I am a switchblade of truth
I lay down in honesty and
remember how the sky starts
to bruise without ever being touched
much like I have done

look at me,
breathing underwater
a tiny pink fist of a lung
gasping for someone to hear her

SUMMER AT MY NANA'S TURQUOISE HOUSE

Laundry taut across the line. Gardens dug and turned until the sun forced us still. Tomatoes, zucchinis and my blood on the fence. Pumpkins and corn. A greenhouse that smells of dirt and decay – floorboards soft beneath my feet, *like they too are giving in.* Blueberries. Raspberries – red as the shame that my dad doesn't call. Morning glories, sunflowers, marigolds. A sky so blue it doesn't wonder what it's like to be anything else. White fence, white clouds, white lightning. Father, son and the holy ghost.

INĦOBBOK

I bend over the old pine table and
roll my Nanu's cigarettes – my tapered hands
lulled by the rhythm of lick and roll,   *lick and roll* –

the paper   thin as the daylight tumbling
through the open window. The cuckoo clock
stares down, supervising my small wrists

at work.   In the kitchen, my grandparents whisper
in a language still foreign to me.   I slide my tongue
around the quiet of my mouth – making new

shapes to match the words I hear.   Soon,
I buzz from the bits of tobacco I've swallowed
and still   am no closer to the mother tongue –

still don't know the meaning of *inħobbok,* but I do know
the sound of love when I hear it.

CHILDHOOD FRAGMENTS

My cousins are small, blonde birds and I am
not. I am black-feathered and raven-haired, my body
full of wishbones. I want to be part of them –
to be someone else's sister, but they are just another
place I don't belong.

                        A boy puts his hands down my pants –
                        his red jeep too harsh against the darkening
                        sky, me in the backseat looking for stars.
                        When I get home, I try and tell my Barbies
                        but I don't know the words for what I've done.

My uncle is Santa Claus and we pretend we
don't know. The small, green house squeezes
generations together, our bodies chest to chest –
the only time confinement feels good.

                        I am seven and alone, my matchstick legs
                        sticking to the seat of our Volvo. At first,
                        I don't see the man come for me and then his
                        hands are in the car – reaching. I flatten myself
                        against my fear until I realize I can run.

There are rooms in my house that I'm not
allowed in, the carpet too white for my freckled
face. I sneak in when I'm alone and get caught
when I don't put the pillows back right.

        We swing between rusted poles and pump
        our legs so hard the swing set lifts out of the hot
        summer grass. We try to reach for heaven but never
        get high enough to talk to God.

I am fourteen and sleep on my mother's floor,
wedged between the bed and the wall. Every night, she
reaches down and touches my hand. I sleep there for
years.

        I lay my head in my Nana's lap. She prays
        the rosary with one hand and strokes my hair with
        the other. She doesn't know she's medicine
        for all parts of me that ache.

My mom cries in the shower, a broken wail
that sounds like falling. She doesn't know I'm
home, *listening*, my hand on the bathroom door –
my fifteen-year-old body rigid at the sound.

        I skip school and cut holes in the screen
        of my bedroom window – smoking bright, white
        cigarettes through the opening. The cleaning
        lady catches me even though I am a ghost.

SEPTEMBER 1988

You'd know the house by the faded turquoise shingles
lifting like a burden off the bones of the first floor. Turn
right off Main and you'll see the long yard reach

past the house – each blade of grass stretched out in
benediction. A porch, painted white in the belly of a
remembered summer, is chipping away like an old
woman's

memory. There's so much to hang on to. The clematis
creeps across the railing, in full bloom
of the bodies that sit and laugh *(or weep)* in folding chairs,

hands busy with work. Soon, the flowers will turn brown,
death spreading from the top down to the root until they
collapse – breathless from giving

all of themselves away. Jesus sits here too, on the cross
above the creaking door, watching us live our very good
lives. We pray to him, for sun or rain and the neighbour's

sick child – but, we forget to pray for my brother so he
dies and he doesn't come back in spring when the flowers
do.

LAST CHILDHOOD SUMMER

she stands in the doorway, long
light cuts across her thighs just above
her last skinned knee

her scalp crawls with secrets and
the ugly understanding of what it means
to bleed –

she'd sacrifice the water and sky
to stay, but there's no way to barter
her freedom now –

no snap of a wishbone to keep her here

so, she leans against the wood frame,
her thin shadow haunting
the last light of day

BIBLE BELT

Main Street crosses Yonge Street right at the top of town.
It's the same way my index fingers make the sign of the
cross against my flat chest – which is proof I believe in
something.

I feel closest to God when I'm not in church, away from
the ornate voices of the repenting caught in the stained
glass, trying to make themselves beautiful.
I want to be a July body, growing

without permission of priests – childhood sneaking
between the blades of deep grass. I am young, and even so,
I know that holy does not always mean good
no matter how hard we pretend.

I MEASURED MY LIFE IN SUMMERS

and after my thirteenth
I stopped counting –
the gap between my teeth
closing around the late summer heat

when I was twelve
I had a brother
and now I don't

it's too hot and too quiet
maybe that's the way
the world grieves, so

I peel his memory until it's clean –
no depression
no gun

and he is alive next to me
his hair glinting in the sunlight
like there is nothing
to be afraid of

HOW TO ASK FOR HELP

Start smoking at fourteen.
Make sure to get caught.
Skip school.
If no one notices – stop going all together.
Switch schools.
Get a ticket for underage drinking.
Run away.
Steal. Make sure to get caught.
Drink vodka on the way to school.
Have the police find you passed out in a rose bush.
Switch schools. Again.
Date a nineteen-year-old when you're fifteen.
Have him pick you up at the house.
Sneak out for months.
Leave notes so they know how to find you.
Come home with a throat full of hickeys.
Wear a turtleneck half of July.
Tell your mom you're afraid you have AIDS.
Lie about where you're going.
Make sure to get caught.
Run away, again. Don't leave a note.
Take summer school classes. Fail them all.
Switch schools, again.
Leave a hash pipe in your drawer.
Make sure someone finds it.
Steal. From everywhere – every chance you get.
Replace the vodka in the liquor cabinet with water.
Get drunk and call your dad.
Tell him how much you hate him.

Drive without a license.
Go to therapy.
Sleep through the sessions until everyone gives up.

Finally get what you didn't want.

TWO SPARROWS IN A HURRICANE

It was warm for October and I wait for the water
like I wait for my father – breath in a cage
and fingers crossed behind my back –
but he doesn't come, no matter the years I wait.

I watch as the sky turns the colour of an old wound,
thick and purple. I know the rain is coming, fresh
as my shame that even fathers don't stay, and when
the creek rose, the water spread like a secret until
everything tasted like mud.

I look for him in the arms of skinny boys, damp
with promises that I'll finally belong. Lord knows, I'll run
my tongue along anything that looks like love
so, I trade my morality for higher ground and wonder how
I burn when I'm soaked to the bone.

TWO SPARROWS

        my father

does

                  stay and

I

        finally belong

* This erasure poem was composed of redacting portions of the previous poem, allowing a new narrative to emerge from what remains.

SIXTEEN

I carve my name into the walls of the porch,
an old tired thing like me at sixteen, all lean
and uneven – begging someone

to sit with her. There is a nest in the rafters and a raven
brings dinner to her babies – I am not hungry,
but I want a mother

so, I open my mouth and I'm somehow left
to starve again. The wood is peeling and I am lonely, even
when you stroke

my hand. You kiss me deeply and I don't love
you – but I make you think I do, as the wheat grass
crawls towards us.

THE BRAVE ONE

We are seventeen, walking with
our arms looped together like bicycle
chains, until we reach the tight-fisted

corner of Davis & Main. One of us
is high, the other is not,
though we both play the part.

She is not afraid out here in the dark
folds of our long walk home. She doesn't
look behind us. Doesn't walk

the center line of a toothless road
to be further away from the dense line
of trees. Doesn't count steps

to stop her mind from racing. I want to
be this brave beast who owns
the night – sleeping with my windows

open, a bedroom door unlocked. Somehow,
when I'm with her, I start to let go.
It's as if her courage hangs like a star –

a thing I can pluck from the dark. We sleep
like men with nothing to be afraid of –
even with no brass barrel lock

on the basement door.

No bars on windows, no chair wedged under
the slick, round knob leading to my bedroom.
Here –   I'm just girl without a cage.

AN INVENTORY OF NIGHT

Nighthawk, night sky,   night of the living
dead.   Night of cousins tickling messages up
my back.   Nightgown, night light and still
the nightmares creep in.   Night covered in moss,
thick as a labyrinth   and the same way out.
Too young for a nightcap   but not too young
to need one.   Night that thunders, never soothes.
Night song, sing me to sleep so I'm not alone –
O Holy Night.   *The stars are brightly shining.*
Night crawling up my back, like the black strike
of a match.   A flicker.   A flame.
Let there be light.

WHERE IT HURTS WHEN YOU'RE ALIVE

I sit on the old weathered porch, paint peeling
like a sunburn until only wood remains. I carve
my name into the floor – just to prove that I exist

and watch clouds,   shaped like hands,
pray across the horizon. I've never much believed
in God, but I've always believed in the sky,

and no matter which one I lay under,   I'm still
just a sliver of a girl,   growing new skin over old bone
in thick July heat.

Everything aches – the flowers, this land, my
body.   Even shadows crouch beneath trees to escape.
It's as if we've all stopped believing.

I can see it in the long neck of the sweetgrass – everything
forgetting and I know I am next.
But I want to remember I was here, waiting
for a sign   it's safe to bleed.

Part Two

I am lonely, yet not everybody will do. I don't know why, some people fill the gaps and others emphasize my loneliness.

– Anaïs Nin

Part Two

ON THE SIDE OF A COUNTRY ROAD

The sun dropped low, preparing
the goldenrod for rest – the tremble
of evening light pressed against the
wheatgrass making it lay down and weep
beside me.

I used to come here as a child
all lean and free – the dirt under
my nails, black as a catastrophe,
thin wisps of womanhood
trailing down my back.

I am her now, a woman
with regret as long as her shadow
aching for the child who didn't know
what was coming, the light dissolving
around me like a promise.

THE LILAC TREE IS BURNING

half scorched and dying – blackened
limbs grab for my hand
                                      and I pull away.

I am looking for something alive, not
something else to save.

THE WEIGHT OF A MARRIAGE IN TROUBLE

I still think – no, *pray*,
that I can fix us. I kneel in front
of anything holy – trees, water, dirt.

It is silent. And yes, the willow weeps
beside me – quiet as an incantation,
but I am left to comb through this decay alone.

The clematis creeps low across the fence
it, too, trying to escape
all this – leaving
all this leaving

maybe
just maybe
I can leave too.

YOU DON'T HAVE TO BE A SAINT TO TALK TO GOD

Look at me, on my knees, pretending
there is something worth praying for –
the trees bent over me like a congregation
of mourners.

I can smell the spine of the willows –
the grace of their bent bodies above
me as my weight presses into the earth.

I know there is a river close,
but all I see is mud.

THE LAST SUPPER

I look at you across the table,
miles of hard oak between us.
Your knife scratches the enamel
on our wedding plates, leaving
irreparable scars.

You are angry again.
I am too.
Our jaws clench around the reasons
though neither of us care.
Not anymore.

I am already imagining life
without you – stepping out of the wound
before it closes, trapping us
both under the skin.

We tried,   I think.
And maybe you can't put together
what was never whole to start with.
And maybe anyone would grow tired
of apologies and *'I love you's'*
even if our intention was to mean it.

And maybe our bodies already know
we've been left before – we pretend
our childhoods don't have a seat at this table.
They do.
They always do.

And when I tell you it's over
I'm leaving in the morning
your face remembers other goodbyes –
for a brief moment I think I'll stay
but your sadness isn't for me
                          and mine,   not for you.

So,   I slip sideways through a crack
in the door – *boneless as sky*
and when the first tilt of light lands
on my pale skin – I see the strength in what
I've done.

BEFORE & AFTER

A crow slices through the day, wings
wide as a cross, quietly mourning
her dead

she is grief stained, black and feathered
      we both cry,   our bodies bent in sorrow
the hot day pressed into the curve of our spine

we bury and weep
bury and weep

until our soft bones crack
our lives in two

HOLY GROUND

It's not my fault that its doesn't rain,
even though the earth howls for it.   I know

what it's like to *need* like that. I also know,
even if I drop to my knees   and dust kicks up

around me,   the rain still won't come.
I've used this dirty mouth to pray before

    and still,

I couldn't break through the wide ribs
of understanding –   so, I stopped trying.

Maybe the point of kneeling
isn't to get closer to God,   but to dirt –

to get down to roots and rock,   to unearth
my skin and bones from the black soil of this grief.

I'M NOT DYING, IT JUST FEELS LIKE IT

Everything is still –
not even the grass moves
when I breathe, my body
just a corpse in a field
trying to get low enough to escape
the violent heat

       I follow a bead of sweat
       in my mind –
           forehead
               to lip
                     to collarbone
     before it slides off my skin and sinks
     to the earth

I want to sink too,
deeper into the soil – teeth first
           grinning with relief to be part
           of something
               that isn't this air,
                     hanging around me
                       like a fever

A YEAR AFTER OUR DIVORCE
After The Good Fight by Ada Limón

I was barely breathing,
pinned against the truth of what I knew. It was
a tightening just under my breastbone – the same
tender place you'd poke your finger while telling me
it didn't hurt.

But it did. It always did.

I kept thinking about how we saw the warning
signs, but our youth gave us a confidence
we did not earn – this is the way of living things.

I kept thinking about how much we've
changed and I wonder who stopped loving who first?

Many times I tried to change you.
Then me.
Then you again.

I wanted to defend all the ways I kept disappointing
you – but gave up somewhere along the way.
You owed me nothing and it showed.

We started leaving in little ways. We whispered
our cruelty so the neighbours wouldn't hear –
but our resentment hung on the fence
and circled the yard.

[There was no escape]

There were bodies, of course.
You cannot simply destroy a life,
even if it's the only way to survive.
Sometimes saving means killing too.

So that's what I did.
I did it for you too.

I'm not as selfish as you think.

A YEAR AFTER

I was   breathing

         my

         confidence

changed

     I   change

and

we

survive.

* This erasure poem was composed of redacting portions of the previous poem, allowing a new narrative to emerge from what remains.

WILD HORSES

you called out to me once
a growl across a hay field still wet with rain
the heat made us crawl through our memories
digging up the bones of who we used to be
but you must sleep in the bed you made
when there weren't enough ways
to say sorry and mean it

I remember the first time you
touched me and the land got still
the same way it does
when a storm is coming

I counted the number of times
you loved me that night
and when you asked why I wear my hair down
I said –
                'that's what horses do'

                their bodies made of grace,
                thunder-bellied and lithe
                every rung of a rib, born to run

                        and they also won't come
                            when you call.

SO MUCH LIVING TO DO

sometimes, things don't mean anything
and then the Dahlia bud opens like a mouth

        in love, *all wanting* – watching itself be
        born

it just walks right into the day
pink wrists bare for the sun to burn

        I've burned too, but never out in the
        open like that

I'm ashamed at how many times I've had
to be born just so I could live

        how do we name a pain so deep we have
        to die over-and-over just to get through it

tell me I am worth the sun on my skin
without the sting it can leave behind

        tell me I'm beautiful just because I exist –
tell me that's enough

LOVERS IN AUGUST

the evening opened them slowly, the torn
edges of the day falling from a plum-coloured
sky. A storm drags itself across the horizon –
lightning pointing its long fingers west

they laid down on a blanket in the yard, heat
rising off their skin like a secret until they
finally reached through the lean grass in search
of each other

water dropped from heavy clouds, offering
mercy from the heat – but they were a
brushfire of desire and everything burned
but the rain.

THE WAY YOU LOVE ME

I see you in the doorway
leaning against the frame
like it's an old friend
you are slick from work and heat
and the evening sun cuts across the yard
like it's lighting my way to you

you watch me in the garden
on my knees in the dirt
and I don't wonder if I'm beautiful
only what it would feel like to run
my finger along the mantle
of your collarbone
like it's the altar of forgiveness

REASONS I MARRIED MY SECOND HUSBAND
After Because by Ellen Bass

Because my name means nothing in the mouth
of a stranger — but when *he calls me*   it sounds
like silk and lightning.   Sometimes clover.

Because when he touches me,   it's like the lip
of the morning pressing into the small of my back
his hand a cup of want.

Because my sternum   no longer aches —
I can breathe so deep,   every bird in the yard
stills   to feel it.

Because he bought me flowers   every Friday
the year my father died —   just so I'd have
something beautiful to be part of.

Because he gave me a body to worship,   held up
to unflinching light until I could see all the ways
I was already good.

Because every time he holds my face,   in the soft
muzzle of his hands,   I become   a miracle.

BORN IN THE KITCHEN

I slice lemons into whispers and let the juice sting
the tiny cuts where I've chewed the memories
off my fingers.

the open window lets through slanted light
and I bloom again – just like that in front
of all that's left of me.

My husband kisses my bare shoulder and I think
I might cry,   here in the kitchen
with summer gathering   above my upper lip –
thighs sticking together

and in walks love   like I deserved it all along.

Part Three

In the ruins of what was, we find what remains
— Unknown Author

LET THE FIRE COME

Somewhere, deep inside the gold dust of these old
lungs, there is a breath so free it sounds like prayer.
I have lived black and dead; a woman tied
to the stake, fire crawling on its hands and knees
towards her – spitting teeth and song into the fresh
borders where dusk meets dawn.

Don't you believe it? Don't you want to see
me unbuttoning my blouse – anger rattling around
my chest and coughing up gold?

THRESHOLD

Open the door
throw it whole and wide
slam it against the dark sky that hangs
around the yard – stretched out like an omen.

You were scared, I see that – fists clenched
and bleeding from the half moon scars
your fingernails have left.

But, it is your baptism now
step out and wait for the blonde
light of day to find you – soft and unafraid
and it will show you just how sweet
your sin has been.

NOTHING STAYS THE SAME

Everything is changing

[people, flowers, families]

I'm still here

[and that is something I wasn't expecting]

Look at me!
Look what I had to do to survive –
Look at what we've all had to do.

NO ONE'S DAUGHTER

Even now, as the days herringbone
together, I can see her. Time has hardened
her hands into temples, where she prays
to a God she no longer believes in.

Her loose skin snags on a memory and follows
her everywhere. She's done what she can
to escape, only to return *over and over* to a life
she doesn't want.

Like all of us, she came from muscle
and bone – has beat herself until the pulp
showed just trying to get home.

The long, autumn grass is matted down
with the bodies of her dead. I am there, too,
staring at the clouds while God drifts away
from us both.

She hangs on, I let go – first of her hand,
then anything that's left. I wish she would lie
here with me, deep in the field – bury herself
beside me.

Let us be two husked bodies –
the thin grass growing around us
like we are worth being reclaimed,
even if it's not by each other.

WHAT MY FATHER GREW

You plant tomatoes in the boxes on the back
deck and we talk about heirlooms and plums.
We don't talk about why you're always so angry.

We talk about how we need more rain – how the Early
Girls will never survive. We don't talk about your dead
son or how we act like he didn't exist.

We don't talk about your childhood or what it feels like to
grow old all alone. I think of you, in your house –
tomatoes the only friends you've got left.

I want to hold you; tell you there's still time to change –
but, your mood changes *quick as a snake bite* and I'm a child
again trying to figure out what I have done.

So, we talk about tomatoes – Cherry, Roma and Black
Krim, and nothing ever changes. We just get older, then
older still – our relationship left to die on the vine.

NOTES FROM THE BACKYARD

Time is a hummingbird wing,
moving faster than a green
eye can count.

A single rose opens its throat
and asks a question to every bird
in the yard.

How many Thursdays in a life well lived?

ACCEPTANCE WEARS A SUMMER DRESS

I am in a field,   my body flattening the soft grass.
Everything is green, like the house I grew up in. Plants,
    birds, envy.

Summer found its way through the back door, all heat and
thunder – spoiling what was left on the counter. No one
notices the heave

and pucker of curtains, forced by wind to breathe.
It is the only thing that moves besides time. I see it front
of me in the sun-bleached

squares where a smiling family once hung on these walls.
    Now, there is only this long grass and a body
remembering what it's like to live

I forgot how beautifully a field can sing.

THE SPACE BETWEEN DREAMING

Healing begins where the wound was made.
  — *Alice Walker*

It is always the thinnest part of night when
I think of her — skin creased with time and regret,
a generation of stories pressed to her palm. I reach for her
like a rosary and pray to the ache

of her heartbeat, *I have heard it before,* tucked under smooth,
white ribs where I once was alive and breathing — a flutter
of belonging. In my dreams, we are both soft, it's as if time
crawls

backwards and we are new again — willing to see each
other between the muscle of our grief and we slip
like a whisper into forgiveness. But again, the morning
comes and we pass

our anger down like heirlooms until there is nothing left to
give and I am further from the soft skeleton
of her body than I have ever been and wait for her
to reach for me.

DREAMING

I think of her

                    alive and breathing

       and we

           forgive

                    until there is nothing left

* This erasure poem was composed of redacting portions of the previous poem, allowing a new narrative to emerge from what remains.

IN THE LONGING OF THIS BODY

I follow every muscle to its ache
and find my mother there, just as lost
as I have been.

I listen to my bones wilt, a sound as soft
as love and find my father – now everywhere
in death where he couldn't be in life.

My fascia wraps around the grief, *trying to choke
it out* – its own neck bruised as twilight
but the sadness still remains.

Then,
I hear it.

      – the heart flutter of forgiveness,
        deep below my breastbone,
        the pulsing of blood.
        The aliveness of it all.

If I am quiet, it almost sounds like music.

MY FATHER'S GRAVE

In the cemetery, out beyond the bloated church,
the path to you is worn down to the roots.

You've been dead nearly as long as I have –
but I am alive now, and still, you are not.

Those long years were just an open mouth
I crawled into to get away from the light,

so I wouldn't have to count all the things
I had lost. Time, breath, bone.

We were dying together – miles apart, both calling
for our mothers but only one of them came.

There is a large willow at the foot
of your grave, its shade yawning

around you. I only put one foot in,
I don't want to remember

what it's like to live without light.
I still see you everywhere –

in the blue eyes of the river that gurgles
your name, in the strawberry blonde sky

before it collapses into night
and in the long legs of the sunflowers

you planted in the yard, their stems bare
but for the hum of your voice –

the sound pushing its way through
the damp earth, saying

even after all this time,
not even a grave can keep us apart.

FOREST CHURCH

Out behind the church there is a forest fermenting
in moss and song – trees pretty as God. This is the real
place I come to pray.

I have given my grief to these roots, looked down
at decay and saw beauty there too. I watch the bark beetles
and cutworms just go on living and think *why not me?*

I can live too, unburdened as the moss – cradling her face
to the damp day, like the hollowed-out roots, their gnarled
fingers pointing my body home. Alive like the river that

holds my name in her wet throat – a sermon only for me,
saying

>*you are good*
>>*you are good*
>>>*you are good*

THIS MORNING

unfolds itself, slow as a love letter,   the sun lifting
out of the backyard.   I watch the birds groom
each other for the day ahead,   washing each other out
in the open – *the intimacy of it*.

Can you imagine a love like that?

this is how it is sometimes,   me in the kitchen,
standing in soft, buttered light – my husband just watching
me, eyes wet with gratitude,   reminding me
that God exists.

Can you imagine a love like that?

THE SUMMER I BECAME A GOD
After The Summer I Lived as a Wolf by Pippa Little

I knew every dehydrated star by name. The night
birds cry out – owls and herons and I cry back,
wild-like and alive. They try and call me in,
but I don't want to be tamed, not even by them.
I circle the moon, dimpled like the thighs of my
mortal body but without any of the shame. I am just
a woman – turned god, with a spine supple as sin.
I am all the way open – both wind and wild,
the darkness folded into my pocket like a wish.
And when the thickest part of summer ends,
I only half return.

CLEANSE

"No man ever steps into the same river twice, for it's not the same river and he's not the same man"
— Heraclitus

    and you finally surrender to the tide
        as it pulls you away from shore
            black water and a carpet full of stars
                you float on the back of your
        own heartbreak
listening to the moon as it whispers
        love songs into the night sky
            let the water wash the hurt
                from your skin until you are
nothing but everything
        naked under the velvet
            of your own belonging

NOTES & ACKNOWLEDGMENTS

A special thank you to the editors of the following journals and magazines, in which the poems in this book, sometimes in earlier versions or with different titles, first appeared:

Writerly Magazine "How to Surrender"

The King City Mosaic "On the Side of a Country Road and "I Told No One and Still, It Is True"

Viewless Wings Poetry Podcast "Acceptance Wears a Summer Dress"

I am beyond grateful to my teachers for their advice and support throughout the writing of this book. I'd especially like to thank Victoria Erikson for creating a space that allowed me to find my voice and Ollie Schminkey for helping me grow as a writer, and for helping to shape my manuscript with their editing and advice. It is with sincere appreciation to Kimberley Burgess for recognizing my potential early on and for the opportunities you've so generously provided.

And lastly, to my tiny family; Donny, Mason and Lauren – you keep me tethered to this world. Thank you for showing me what unconditional love feels like. The three of you are my *greatest* gift.

Cover artwork is *Trichoglossus Porphyrocephalus, Porphyry Crowned Lorikeet* by John Gould, 1844.

The epigraph used to introduce Part One is from the novel "For One More Day" by Mitch Album

"*September 1988*" is inspired by "At Roane Head" by Robin Roberston in which I borrow and change the opening line *"you'd know her house by"*.

"*Two Sparrows in a Hurricane*" is after the song of the same name by Tanya Tucker.

"*Two Sparrows*" is an Erasure poem from the text of *"Two Sparrows in a Hurricane"* on the previous page.

In the poem *"An Inventory of Night"* the line "O-Holy Night, the stars are brightly shining" is from the song *"O-Holy Night"* by Placide Cappeau, 1843.

The epigraph used to introduce Part Two is a diary entry by Anaïs Nin.

"*A Year After Our Divorce*" is after Ada Limón's poem *"The Good Fight"*

"*A Year After*" is an Erasure poem from the text of *"A Year After Our Divorce"* on the previous page.

"*Reasons I Married My Second Husband*" is after Ellen Bass's poem *"Because"*.

The opening line of *"Reasons I Married My Second Husband"* was inspired by a line from the song *"Solitude"* by Black Sabbath.

The epigraph used to introduce Part Three is from an Unknown Author.

The epigraph at the beginning of *"The Space Between Dreaming"* is from the book *"The Way Forward is with a Broken Heart"* by Alice Walker

"Dreaming" is an Erasure poem from the text of *"The Space Between Dreaming"* on the previous page.

"The Summer I Became a God" is after Pippa Little's poem *"The Summer I Lived as a Wolf"*

The epigraph at the beginning of *"Cleanse"* originates from the ancient Greek philosopher Heraclitus of Ephesus.

www.ingramcontent.com/pod-product-compliance
Lightning Source LLC
Chambersburg PA
CBHW010248010526
44119CB00055B/777